What others are saying about this book:

"Not only does Kalyn Wolf Gibbens offer some good advice, her writing style is enjoyable and pulls the reader into the book...great sense of humor!"

Patricia Skovgaard
Married, December 1993

"I have read *Marrying Smart!* and enjoyed it immensely. I am giving a copy to our daughter. I know she will be ecstatic in reading and using the magnificent suggestions for creating and attracting her ideal mate."

Lew Epstein,
Founder of the Lew Epstein Men and Women's Clubs

"Kalyn Wolf Gibbens lovingly weaves her personal journey to finding her heart's desire with practical tools she offers to others who want to "marry smart"... This little book (with a big heart) is a testament to her personal commitment to reducing the 55% divorce rate in the U.S. by helping people find the "right" person to marry in the first place. She encourages us all to take full responsibility for healing ourselves from dysfunctional family patterns, giving the next generation of children the gift of healthier role models for loving, committed relationships."

Todd Peterson,
Counselor in Private Practice

"I found Kalyn's book, *Marrying Smart!*, positive and hopeful. She offers good details for organization and follow through. I very much enjoyed her ideas and found the book very engaging."

Charlotte Peterson, Ph.D

"Written in a personal style with tangible steps you can follow, this book is an open, honest breath of fresh air. If you've felt discouraged about achieving a healthy, loving commitment, Kalyn's words will reawaken faith and hope."

Rev. Danahy Sharonrose, MA, MFCC

About the author:

Kalyn Wolf Gibbens lives in Eugene, OR with her husband and twin children. In conjunction with her dual roles as wife and mother, she is an entrepreneur, lecturer, publisher, community member

Kalyn Wolf Gibbens

and world citizen. Kalyn is a catalyst for connection. Wherever she goes, be it in business or personal relationships she leaves the people she meets making connections on a level they didn't see possible. Kalyn's hope is that everyone who reads her book is empowered with the understanding of who they are and what they can accomplish. Her personal commitment to seeing the divorce rate drop from it's current 55% is a testament to her commitment and zest towards life. Before becoming an author Kalyn enjoyed success as a make-up artist for film and theater, an artist's model, body worker, and owner of a flotation tank center in Tucson, Arizona. She has traveled extensively throughout India, Thailand, Greece, Israel, The United States and Canada creating lasting relationships wherever she goes.

Marrying Smart!

A Practical Guide For Attracting Your Mate

Kalyn Wolf Gibbens

Marrying Smart!
A Practical Guide For Attracting Your Mate
by Kalyn Wolf Gibbens

Published by: **Just Your Type**
Publishing & Marketing
P.O. Box 5931
Eugene, OR 97405
(503) 683-4149

Copyright © 1994 Kalyn Wolf Gibbens
First printing 1994
Printed in the United States of America

J   I   H   G   F   E   D   C   B   A

Cover Illustration by Peter McCallum
Index by Ritch Pope
Typesetting & Book Design by Just Your Type

Library of Congress Catalog Card Number 94-075125

Publisher's Cataloging in Publication

Gibbens, Kalyn Wolf.
    Marrying smart : a practical guide for attracting your mate / by Kalyn Wolf Gibbens.
    p. cm.
    Includes bibliographical references and index.
    ISBN 1-884517-15-3

    1. Marriage--United States. 2. Mate selection--United States.
3. Man-woman relationships.   I. Title.

HQ734.G1994   306.81
                                   QB194-95

This book has been passed by the Literature Review Office at the Bahá'í National Center, Wilmette, Illinois, December 20, 1993

The content of this book has been printed on recycled paper.

Dedicated with love to my children Elias and Anaia, my husband Doug, and especially to my grandmother Hanna Wolf who supported me during my efforts.

THE FINE PRINT

This publication is designed to provide accurate and authoritative information with regard to the subject matter covered. It is sold with the understanding that the publisher is not engaged in rendering legal, accounting, or other professional advice. If legal advice or other expert assistance is required, the services of a competent professional person should be sought.

CONTENTS

FOREWORD

In September 1993, a friend called to tell me her firm was reviewing a book written by our mutual friend, Kalyn Gibbens. Three years earlier, Kalyn had told me that she intended to write a book on how to prepare for marriage and find an ideal mate. I was happy to hear that she had finished the book.

My friend said she had seen a copy of the book and that Kalyn had shared many good pieces of advice in it. I called Kalyn later that week and asked if she would send me a proof copy. As I read the book, I found insights and thought-stirring passages on every page. One sitting was all I needed to read from cover to cover. I couldn't put it down. When I finished the last page, I immediately called Kalyn to thank her for her wonderful work and tell her about the impact it had on me.

I was on the verge of letting go of the last strands of a relationship that had haunted me for three years when I read Marrying Smart. Afterwards, Kalyn and I talked at great length about finding happiness, about moving into a place of certainty and commitment in my life and DOING something about it. I agreed to give her system a shot. What did I have to loose? I knew that no matter what, I would end up a happier person. The heart of Kalyn's system, after all, is not about being married. It is about being happy. I remembered talking with another friend a few months earlier; she had suggested that I focus not on finding a mate, but rather on finding my heart's desire. After much thought I realized that my heart's desire was to be happy. Kalyn's book came at the right time. I saw it as a tool to help me begin working toward my heart's desire. Perhaps marriage would be a part of that happiness, perhaps not. Either way, I was determined to begin the journey.

Kalyn agreed to be my relationships coach and I used the system outlined in her book. I set a date, made my list and ritualistically read my list, burned it, and sent the ashes off into the night sky. Then, a funny thing happened: I felt a calm certainty about marriage that I had never felt before. I felt as if I were already married and all I had to do was find my mate. Weird. Reading my list aloud three times a day for three days—three pages of characteristics and qualities that I wanted in a mate—helped me see that I was not looking for Mr. Perfect. Three weeks later on a business trip abroad a friend of mine introduced me to a business contact of hers. Three months later he became my husband.

I must say that I was one of Kalyn's skeptical friends who did not believe that one could use a systematic approach to find lasting love and a good mate (of course I never told her that until recently). When Kalyn first told me about her system, and that the first step was to set a date by which she would be married, I was worried. It seemed too business-like for me. How could such timeline planning leave room for the fairy tale romance that is meant to be part of courtship and marriage? Enlisting the support of friends in order to find a life companion seemed dangerous to me—like setting herself up with too many expectations. After all, aren't we all told that love comes when you least expect it? The last thing I wanted Kalyn to do—or myself or any of my other single friends—was to have too many expectations. I thought planning for love and marriage, expecting it, would take away the necessary element of surprise that would guarantee its arrival. I didn't think Kalyn's system would work for her or anyone else. I was certain that she would find herself disappointed when her "married by" date came around and she was still single. On December 17, 1989 I was pleasantly proven wrong. That is the day Kalyn married Doug Gibbens. On December 27, 1993 I was again pleasantly proven wrong—that is the day I married the man I met abroad. We have become best friends and best loves. I have learned that expecting love is one of the best ways to find it because after all the world does live up to all our expectations.

If you are searching for happiness, I encourage you to read Kalyn's book. Whether you want to be married or not, Kalyn offers good advice for anyone who desires happiness. Expect it.

Patricia Skovgaard,
Heidelberg, Germany

A NOTE FROM KALYN

Y ou will find this book is written differently
from other books of its kind. When I was
reading "how to" books on relationships, I
always wondered what kind of relationship the author was
in; I'd say to myself, "This is great in theory, but does it work
in practice?" Sometimes I would get really excited about
following the advice of some authority only to find out later
that not only had they never been married, but they had
never even been in a long term committed relationship! I
want you to know that I have lived this plan that I am now
revealing to you. This isn't just some theory I thought
could work under ideal circumstances. The plan I devised
worked for me, and it can work for you too.

I have read books that recommend everything from finding your romantic victim's favorite sexual act and skillfully performing it, to changing your hair color, your eye color, your personality, even your *sex* in order to manipulate some fool into falling in love with you.

You will **not** receive that kind of advice in this book. I respect you and your partner too much for that kind of nonsense. What you will receive by reading this book is a goal setting plan that will take you through your engagement with some sensible advice about making your marriage a lasting union.

You will:

- Ask yourself why you want to get married.
- Declare your wedding date.
- Write down your goal.
- Take responsibility for your future.
- Decide what attributes you want your mate to possess.
- Discover the qualities you bring to a relationship.
- Establish credibility for yourself by keeping your commitments.
- Explore ways to put yourself in the right marketplace to find your mate.
- Take responsibility for your past relationships.
- Find the trust it takes to have faith in the Universe.
- Marry Smart!

I firmly believe that unless you can be honest, forthright, and **totally yourself** in a relationship, it is best not to be in one. I spent many years turning myself into a pretzel listening to advice from people who had no right giving it. I finally got fed up, and decided to listen to my own inner voice, live my life with integrity, and search out kindred spirits. It is to these kindred spirits, that I write this book.

I also want you to know that I am not Madison Avenue's idea of the perfect looking woman. I tell you this because I feel it is very important that you know you do not have to have fabulous looks to be attractive. Some of the most beautiful people I know would be considered plain by Hollywood standards. What is important is that you feel good about yourself, that you show your best attributes and that you find inner beauty and peace about your outward appearance.

I have written this book in two parts: First, you will see the instruction, printed in plain type; second, you will read how I put that instruction to work in my own life, which is printed in italics. I have told the truth, the whole truth, and nothing but the truth, so help me God, no matter what the embarrassment. I hope you enjoy reading my story, but more importantly, I wish you good luck and happiness with your plan and your adventure of life.

In A Nutshell

I married Douglas Gibbens on December 17, 1989. This was after a 16 month plan I devised with the intent of being married by the end of 1989. On Labor Day Weekend 1988, I went to a conference in San Francisco for singles. There, I kid you not, I was giving a seminar about affection and the abstaining adult. I met a man who asked me if I wanted to be married (not to him—just in general). I gave him my best "spiritual" answer, "If it's God's will". He told me he gleaned from my answer that I was ambiguous about being married and until I was firm in my conviction, I would remain single. He told me that God did indeed want me to marry and the only thing getting in my way, was me. I thought about this long and hard. He was right. So that day, September 9, 1988, I decided that I wanted to be married, and knowing a bit about goal setting, I decided to put a date on it: I would be married by the end of 1989.

On my way home I started making a plan of action. I had accomplished a lot in my life, and I thought that as an experiment, I would set out to meet this goal the same way I had the others. I knew that if I were to marry it would take a group effort to pull it off. I told all my friends of my intentions and asked them to put energy and prayers toward my goal. I got lots of reactions, everything from tremendous support to tremendous opposition.

I let nothing stop me. During this period of time it was as though I was in a bubble of positive action. Rejection did not exist. If I dated someone who didn't want me, I saw it as a relief and a confirmation that they just weren't the "right" one. When I dated someone who I knew was inappropriate, I stopped dating them. My life transformed in the most wonderful way. I no longer wanted to change anyone. I was looking for my mate as is...just like they would get me.

I believe the steps I took to get married can be learned. Therefore people who are in the same position I was in can successfully find themselves in a fulfilling, happy marriage. I have given my plan to several people over the past few years. For the most part, those who have followed it now find themselves either happily married, on their way to marriage, or happily single. Those who haven't followed the advice are still single and complaining about it.

ACKNOWLEDGMENTS

There are many people I want to thank for supporting me in writing this book and achieving my goal: Rayna Dorsey, for sitting with me and contributing her time and ideas–without her I wouldn't have started the book; Judy Lindsey, my relationships coach; Jack Derby for giving me the list portion of the plan; Patricia Skovgaard; Sue Bingham; Jim and Cherie Sohnen-Moe; the entire North Pima County Bahá'í Community; the Tucson Chapter of The Lew Epstein Men and Women's Club, for being my support system, believing in me, and not acting too shocked when I accomplished my goal; Gina Mendello; Rich Landergren; and all my friends who encouraged me to write this book so they could read it; Lew and Francine Epstein, for introducing me to the idea of having compassion for men, while gently and humorously empowering me in the practice of the equality of men and women. Brian Redfield and Rosemarie Atensio for their invaluable assistance. To Red Grammer for giving me the love of the Bahá'í Faith. To Douglas Gibbens, my husband and father of our twin children, Elias and Anaia, thank you. Without you this couldn't have been done. I thank God everyday for allowing us to find each other. You are my partner, and my best dream. I love you.

And most importantly to Bahá'u'lláh, the Prophet-founder of the Bahá'í Faith. Through him I found my faith, my love and my life.

Marrying Smart!

CHAPTER ONE

ARE YOU SURE YOU WANT TO BE MARRIED?

B eing married is a serious commitment. There are times when it is wonderful and times when it is not so wonderful. When it is wonderful marriage is boundless. You experience the highest highs when you are fully at peace and at one with your partner. At those times you don't need a commitment to want to stay together. The commitment kicks in when times are not so wonderful, and believe me, there will be those times.

In the first six weeks of marriage, I was sure I had made the mistake of my life. I wasn't used to this new person in my home and I didn't necessarily want him there 24 hours a day 60 seconds a minute. It took commitment, work and patience to work out the details of our marriage.

You need to ask yourself if you really understand the seriousness of the commitment you are about to undertake. When you are single there is no one else you have to consult about anything. If you want to go to a movie, you go. If you want to see a friend after work and have dinner, you do it. If you want to have friends or family over to your house, you invite them. After you marry, there is another person to consider, and a certain amount of your freedom will have to be viewed from a new vantage point—that of a couple. This is not necessarily a burden—in itself it can be a new found freedom. You also have your days and nights to share with someone you know truly cares about you, and what it is you have to say. When times are intimate, there is nothing better than to be with that one special person you have chosen to spend your life with. And when children come...well, let's say you will never see your spouse in the same light again.

*Before Doug and I married we discussed many things like how many children we wanted, our philosophy of raising them, what we thought of all our relatives, what part we saw them playing in our lives and so on. Perhaps the most important subject we considered however was the quality of our commitment. When we entered our marriage we resolved ourselves to this being **it**. After I got pregnant the commitment deepened even more. Nothing prepared us, however, for what* *happened to us during childbirth. During that process I fell in love with Doug all over again. The delivery was complicated and Doug was there 1000% the whole time. After we all came home from the hospital, I was still fairly ill and he kept night watch every night so I could get some sleep. He staved off unhelpful guests and relatives...I swear if he had breasts he would have nursed those babies himself. My point is that his commitment really kicked in. He proved himself beyond measure during that time and others too numerous to go into here—after all, this chapter is not about how wonderful Doug is—it is about asking yourself some pretty tough questions, such as:*

What can I accomplish as a married person that I can't as a single person? Are there other ways I can accomplish these tasks or goals?

I felt I had done all the growing I could as a single person and marriage was the next step in my personal evolution. Given my values, I needed to get married to start a family and have children. I wanted a life mate I could trust, to be intimate with and grow with, both separately and as a unit.

There are many reasons to get married. Some of the popular ones are: To have company around; to get regular sex; to fulfill the status quo; to have children; to get out of a small town; and because either you or your partner is pregnant.

Marriage is a big step and if you have a commit-

31

ment to well-being you might want to investigate **your** reasons. If, for example, you feel you want to marry only to save yourself from an unhappy situation–show some backbone and move out of it yourself! True marriage, the kind I'm talking about in this book is not about being "saved" by someone. Do yourself a favor and save yourself. That action will in itself save you heartache in the long run.

Whatever your reasons to marry are, step back and look at them objectively. If they include goals that are better served outside of marriage, start accomplishing those goals today. Divorce in this country is at such epidemic proportions, that I have made a personal commitment to see the divorce rate decline from it's current 55% to 20% by the year 2000. One of the best ways to help the divorce rate drop is by marrying the "right" person. This book is written to intelligent, caring, devoted and committed people who want to make a difference in the state of matrimony in their personal lives. If this is the kind of marriage you are looking for go on to Chapter Two. If however after reading Chapter One you've decided this kind of relationship is not for you yet, close the book, read it when you are ready, or give it to a friend.

CHAPTER TWO

FINDING YOUR IDEAL MATE IS EASIER THAN YOU THINK.

W hat do you want? Take this time to make a written statement of what you want, in your own words, in a positive form. The statement is a written assertion of a task that will be completed by the date you set. My statement was:

"I, Kalyn, will be married by the end of 1989."

This is a very important part of the process. You are making a commitment with absolutely no evidence that you will accomplish it. I understand it's hard enough to make a promise when you know you can keep it, but to do so when you aren't sure can feel crazy. If you feel you're going out on a limb by doing this, think about the people who signed and supported the Declaration of Independence. By just the action of their word, those people changed the history of the world. What you are doing is changing the course of your personal history.

Many people know what they want but stop there. They think if they wish for it, it will happen. And it might. Then again, it might not. In my experience, making a "Declaration of Intent to Marry" is a powerful tool. Therefore when you take this step stay in reality. If you give yourself two months to marry you will most probably be disappointed (that is, of course, unless you are already engaged or otherwise involved). Give yourself at least one year, four seasons, to accomplish this task.

I gave myself 16 months. On Labor Day weekend 1988, I declared that I would be married by the end of 1989. I made that declaration with no evidence that it could be done. I had no prospects. My wedding was December 17, 1989. Remember, you are attracting your mate—the one you will share your life with forever. Don't rush it.

Now that you've put things into perspective, write your declaration and go on to Chapter Three.

Declaration Worksheet

N ow it's your turn. This might be a big step for you but I promise it won't hurt. Go ahead, get your pen.

I _____
Your Name

will be married by _____
Month, Day, Year

CHAPTER THREE

WHAT IS YOUR WORTH?

What are you worth? I don't mean in dollars and cents. I mean, what are you bringing to your marriage? What attributes do you offer to your mate? This is a vital question to ask yourself when you want to have a healthy relationship. What are the personality traits that make you the package you are. Doug always tells me what a "good deal" I got in marrying him and he's right. He knows his worth. Do you think you are a "good deal"? I suggest listing your attributes. Don't be shy. There is great freedom in knowing who you are. I also suggest being honest with yourself, after all no one else needs to see this list but you.

Let's get the physical stuff out of the way first. If

you feel good about your appearance write that down on your list. Feeling good about your appearance is an asset to your personality and sexuality. No one, and I mean **no one** enjoys hearing their loved one complaining about their appearance. It is not cute, it is not sexy, it is not attractive, it is not the truth. If you do not feel good about yourself physically do something about it. A hint: this has very little to do with your actual looks and a lot to do with how you feel about them.

*When I was in college, an art teacher asked me to model for him. After I turned sixteen shades of red I politely said something like, "I'd rather jump from Niagara Falls...you pervert." My reaction startled me. Being a self examining sort of person I started asking myself why I would have that kind of feeling about being nude. When I was in my early 20's I was a **very** confrontive person with myself, so I called a local art modeling agency and asked if they needed any models. They said no, I said thank you and hung up the phone relieved that I wouldn't have to confront the issue just yet. For the next six months I asked everyone I met how they felt about their body. Now I realize that my survey was not done under very scientific conditions but this is what I found out: 97% of the people I interviewed thought there was something to improve in their appearance; 80% wanted to lose weight; 15% wanted to gain weight; 60% thought there must be some-*

thing they could do to improve their appearance as far as using a different kind of make-up or growing a beard, etc.; 35% thought that working out would help; 15% wanted corrective surgery. Then I found out something that frankly surprised me—the more typically gorgeous the person I interviewed was—the worse they felt about themselves. The more average looking a person was—the better they felt about themselves physically. I was enlightened by my casual study. After six months passed I felt much better about myself. I began modeling shortly thereafter. My physical appearance hadn't altered at all. It was the mental image I had of myself that transformed.

How are you at housekeeping? Are you tidy or messy? Are you clean, enjoy a well lived in quality to your home or do you live in squalor? Do you enjoy the effect of fresh flowers in your home? Do plants thrive around you or do you tend to kill them? How about money? How do you feel about money? The amount of money you are in possession of does not count here. Some of the most wealthy people I know are also the biggest tightwads. How generous are you with the money you have? How loyal are you? How good a listener? Do you care for animals and trees? Do you recycle? How's your sense of humor, your sense of adventure? Are you a risk taker? Are you musically inclined? Do you like to dance? How important is reading in your life? How important is spirituality in your life? Do you enjoy the outdoors? Have you had an experience with extraterrestrial life forms? What are the skills that you have mastered that have made you successful? What do you consider to be your faults? What are you committed to in your life? Get the picture? Write all of these characteristics down. They compile the list of your self-worth, your self-esteem. Wherever you go, this list goes with you. Now when you meet someone, you will know what you bring to a relationship. You will know your worth.

Self-worth List

What I Bring To A Relationship

N ow it's your turn to put your likes, dislikes, attributes, habits, goals, commitments, dreams, fears and hopes down on paper. This could take some time. Unless you have done some self examination prior to reading this book it could take a lot of time. Do yourself a favor and don't rush it. This is a vital step in understanding what you have to offer in life, and what you offer to a mate. Just write what you feel. You may be surprised at what comes up. You can make copies of the blank list pages if you need more space. Write as little or as much as feels comfortable to you. The list starts on the next page...

What I have to offer in a _____

relationship: _____

_____ _____

_____ _____

_____ _____

_____ _____

_____ _____

_____ _____

_____ _____

_____ _____

_____ _____

_____ _____

_____ _____

_____ _____

_____ _____

What I Bring To A Relationship

_____   _____

_____   _____

_____   _____

_____   _____

_____   _____

_____   _____

_____   _____

_____   _____

_____   _____

_____   _____

_____   _____

_____   _____

_____   _____

_____   _____

_____   _____

_____   _____

_____   _____

_____   _____

_____   _____

_____   _____

_____   _____

_____   _____

_____   _____

_____   _____

_____   _____

_____   _____

_____   _____

_____   _____

_____   _____

_____   _____

_____   _____

_____   _____

_____   _____

_____   _____

_____   _____

CHAPTER FOUR

What Does Your Ideal Mate Look Like?

This step is two fold. The first is to choose your mate's attributes from the universal menu of life. The second is to create a point of reference. This step is perhaps the most fun you will have during this whole process (except of course when you see the faces of your friends and relatives when you announce your wedding date).

Write down everything, and I mean everything, you want. Be sure to state the attributes in positive, present tense. For example, he or she is trustworthy, kind, free from smoke, etc. One hint: Unless it is extremely important that your mate look a certain way (i.e., blond, dark, tall, zaftig...), leave out any physical requirements

except that they be attractive to you. I mean let's face it, if your intended doesn't "bake your cookies" what good is the rest of the list? By limiting your mate to any specific physical requirements you really only limit your choices and your results.

When I was in college, I found myself extremely attracted to a man I would never have guessed I'd be attracted. He was 2 inches shorter than me, balding, freckled, a character actor type, and one of the sexiest men with whom I've ever been in contact. In contrast, Doug is 6 feet 2 inches, 235 pounds, and quite frankly a hunk. My point is, you never know to whom you will be attracted.

Do you think Elizabeth Taylor dreamed of a husband who looked like Mike Todd, or Julia Roberts longed for a man who looks like Lyle Lovett? Perhaps...but I doubt it. Besides looks' fade...teeth can fall out, hair can recede, skin wrinkles, physical attributes fall and fade, but that basic personality lives on and intensifies with time and age.

On my list, which was 2 1/2 pages long, I included that he be trustworthy, free from smoke, alcohol, and enjoy his life's work. It took me all of one day to write my initial list. Then I started refining it. Actually, I mostly added to it.

This is your time to ask for anything you want. Just remember–the way the universe works you will probably get it. The completion of this list may take a few days. When you feel it is complete–prioritize your list. Emphasize the top five or so attributes. This is important for future reference. Be sure to include on your list all the qualities you want your mate to possess, no matter how petty you might think they are.

Now for part two: If you are anything like me, your past includes a few lousy relationships. My guess is that part of the reason for these disasters is that you didn't know what you wanted and/or you weren't getting what you needed from the person. So, you sabotaged the relationship to get out of it. You know those priorities you have? When you start dating someone, check them against your list. If they don't possess all of the top five attributes STOP DATING THEM!!!

I dated a *guy who had four out of the top five qualities. He didn't want children. I stopped dating him as soon as I found out that information. He is a good acquaintance, but was not marriage material for me. I didn't want to feel I had to change anyone. And I knew there were plenty of men out there who would fit my requirements.*

At this point let me tell you a little metaphor my grandmother used when she spoke of men. "Men" she said, "Are like buses, there's always another one coming down the street."

I know this sounds crass, but applied to men or

women the theory really holds water. Bear with me—you're sitting at a bus stop waiting for a bus to take you to the east side of town. Along comes a bus that is unmarked and, if you are a careful person, you would ask the bus driver what direction the bus is going. He or she says, it is going north. You wouldn't get on the bus would you? Of course not. You would wait for another bus that would take you to your destination. It might be the next bus, or it might be the third bus, but you would wait until the appropriate bus came along before you boarded. Let's say you don't ask the driver which direction the bus is heading. You just get on. About five minutes into the ride, when it becomes clear that bus is not going in your direction, wouldn't you get off the bus? Now, of course, some people get on the first bus they find. They just ride around for the fun of it, or ride around complaining about never getting where they want to go. Worse, some just stay confused about their situation and keep going in circles. If you find yourself in that situation, GET OFF THE BUS! Give up your seat to someone who wants to be there.

If you want to go somewhere in a relationship and you do not have complete alignment from the other person, you could end up in a totally different place than you want to be. Now, if you are into chance, this could be quite exciting. However, if you have a direction it will eventually frustrate you, and you will resent it. Trust me.

Back to the original story. The truth is, I wasn't right for this guy. So, instead of dating each other for six months, having a great time and ultimately breaking up with tears and bad feelings, we got to acknowledge our differences and remain friendly.

I know, you might say, "But what if he changed his mind about having children?" I had to take that risk. The chances were just as great that he wouldn't have changed. I would have wasted at least six months and probably some of my self-esteem.

In the past, based on your emotions, you were probably not trustworthy to make smart choices in the area of relationships. In prioritizing your list by naming the top five attributes you give yourself a FAIL SAFE METHOD to keep that from ever happening again. A checks and balance system if you will.

Recently, someone asked me what happens if the person they are dating fulfills their top five requirements but comes from a dysfunctional family and has problems because of that. My best answer is this: Assume everyone you date comes from a dysfunctional family. The odds are pretty good that they do. If they don't they are an anomaly and will eventually have to deal with the dysfunctional family you probably come from. My point is this:

Whether or not they come from a dysfunctional family is not the best question you can ask yourself. A better question is...can you help them to foster their positive qualities and can you live with their bad habits. Remember, one man's ceiling is another man's floor, and there is no telling what wonderful qualities a person carries until they feel nurtured and loved. That goes for you too.

Have fun writing your list, and NEVER, EVER, EVER compromise on your top five. If your date doesn't possess those attributes now, leave them alone. Their values are just as important to them as yours are to you. Trying to change someone doesn't work. If you don't believe me, read "Women Who Love Too Much", by Robin Norwood (regardless of your gender). In that book Ms. Norwood more than adequately illustrates the dangers of getting involved in a co-dependent relationship. Or rather, a relationship in which you believe the person you are involved with wouldn't be so bad if only they had you in their life to straighten them out.

ATTRIBUTE LIST

GO FOR IT!

My mate is: _____   _____

_____   _____

_____   _____

_____   _____

_____   _____

_____   _____

_____   _____

_____   _____

_____   _____

_____   _____

_____   _____

_____   _____

_____   _____

_____   _____

_____   _____

_____   _____

_____   _____

_____   _____

_____   _____

_____   _____

_____   _____

_____   _____

_____   _____

_____   _____

_____   _____

_____   _____

And the top five attributes are:

1. _____

2. _____

3. _____

4. _____

5. _____

CHAPTER FIVE

THIS SIMPLE SECRET GUARANTEES SUCCESS...
IF YOU DO IT!

Are you ready? Okay, here it is, Read your list aloud three times a day for three days, then burn it. Okay, so it sounds ooga booga, but it works! Just look at it as a symbolic gesture.

It took me three attempts to accomplish this step, so be compassionate and patient with yourself. The first time I attempted this step, I got to the second day and "forgot" to say it the third time. The second attempt, I skipped a day. The third attempt was the winner. On the morning of Wednesday, April 19, 1989 (six weeks after I wrote my list), I read the list out loud with passion and confidence that I would accomplish my task this time. All went well. I was feeling strong, happy and I actually felt as though I was somehow calling my mate to me—kind of like giving my order to the cosmic waiter.

On Friday, I left work to enjoy a two day vacation. At 9:00pm, one of my employees called to tell me he couldn't work Saturday. I had promised my other employee the day off. That left me having to go into the office the next day. I was bummed. I went to my room to read aloud the list for the final time and remembered I had left my date book and the list at the office. Well, I had it set up in my mind that if I couldn't stick with this simple commitment I didn't deserve to get married. Besides, I was so close to finishing the step and I didn't want to start from scratch again. I got in the car, drove 20 miles to work and back home again, stood on my balcony on a beautiful, clear, warm desert night at 10:00pm, read my list with all my heart and soul, then burned it in an abalone shell. The next morning I woke up refreshed and happy; then I remembered I had to go to work. I owned a flotation tank and relaxation center. I got to the office around 10:00am, and found one message on the answering machine. A new customer wanted to come in, so we made an appointment for 10:30. When he walked through the door I felt incredible compassion for him. He had a wonderful smile, and I thought he was really cute, but he looked like he was in a lot of pain. His back was beaten up from his job. I gave him 45 minutes with a relaxation machine but only charged him for 20. This was unlike me. We talked about the equality of men and women, *and nature of the universe in regard to relationships. He told me he was living with a married woman who was estranged from her husband. He told me they were having a lot of problems and he was having a difficult time sorting things out. I told him that the relationship was totally inappropriate and suggested he might be happier being with a woman who would be committed only to him. When he left, I felt really good about our session. I didn't hear from him again until September, months after he broke up with the married woman. I married him in December. When I met Doug he possessed 85% of the qualities on my list and all top five attributes.*

By following this step completely, you are following through on a commitment. The message seeps into your internal program that you are capable of keeping your word. If you cannot complete this simple commitment, will you be able to put forth the energy it takes to make a marriage? Looking at a list every day is admirable, but until you carry your requirements with you, in your body and mind, the transformation will not occur. By reading your list aloud for three days, you are burning it into your memory. What you are doing here is becoming a person who will attract these qualities in a mate. When you become that person, your mate will show up. So, don't just read your list, internalize it. Read it with passion and know for certain that you deserve it, and you will receive those qualities in your mate.

Burning the list is significant, it releases and transforms the energy. Native Americans burn their prayer ties so that the smoke will carry their prayer to the Creator. In essence, you are doing the same. You are releasing your list to the Universe so that it may return to you in the form of a mate. If you don't have a fireplace, you can burn it over a sink, in a shell or in a campfire. Be aware of your safety and the safety of your surroundings. Oh yeah, don't stand too close to a smoke detector.

CHAPTER SIX

Keeping This Secret Could Lead To Failure!

Tell everyone about your goal. The more you say your goal, the more "real" it will be to you. The most important people to say it to are your dates. I suggest waiting no longer than the third date. Depending on their reaction, you will be able to know their intentions. I know this sounds bold, but we are not fooling around here. If you want to be married—you have to tell people about it, after all you never know who might know your "spouse to be."

I told everyone I knew. I always said it with sincerity and conviction. When my younger sister got married, eleven weeks before me, I wasn't engaged yet. In fact Doug and I weren't even in a committed relationship yet, in fact, we had *only been on three dates. Someone at the wedding asked me that potentially embarrassing and awful question. "So Kalyn, when are **you** getting married?" After my initial shock (I couldn't believe anyone would be that tactless) I said, "By the end of '89." He remarked that he didn't know I was engaged. When I informed him I wasn't, he looked at me sideways, said something I don't remember, turned around and walked away. I could only imagine the look on his face when he received an announcement to my wedding eight weeks later.*

When I would bring up the subject of marriage on dates, I got a variety of responses—everything from, "That's nice...it's been good knowing you...good-bye," to "Maybe you shouldn't tell that to people so early in a relationship," to Doug's response..."Sounds good to me"!

I was inspired to create this step by a girlfriend who was jilted. She thought she was going to marry this fellow after he spent four years in Africa. For four years they wrote to each other, declaring their love, saying they would marry when he returned. Then, on the day he was supposed to come home, she received one final letter. He decided to stay in Africa and marry someone else. She was devastated. A few months later, she met someone else. They dated platonically for a couple of months, and then one night he kissed her. The next day she called him to inform him that she was not looking for another "boyfriend", and if he wasn't looking for a relationship that might lead to marriage, she'd rather not see him again. They married six months later. **Yes**, this step is frightening. **Yes**, it is bold. **Yes**, it works and may save you from wasting precious time.

CHAPTER SEVEN

CUTTING THE MUSTARD

Y ou have to be willing to do whatever it takes to accomplish your goal. Now, when I say this, I want to be clear that I mean anything that is not unscrupulous. I believe it is inappropriate to break up someone's marriage so you can get married. I also believe it is inappropriate to kill a friendship to date your best friend's partner. What I mean by this step is quite simple; there are things you can do to meet people that are relatively safe and at the same time just a bit risky. Personal ads are a wonderful resource for dating. I highly recommend both placing and answering personal ads. I have eight friends who met their mates that way. Joining a class or a club that is of interest to you will help you meet new people. It also gives you common ground with these new prospects. Blind dates from friends and family (perhaps the most confronting way to meet someone), work for some people. My Mom and Dad, for instance, met on a blind date. Join a singles' club, or kill two birds with one stone and enjoy a Club Med type vacation. Carry business cards. Use business as a way to meet people.

Once I gave my business card to a man at the health food store. Feeling cocky, I commented that someday he would be happy to have it. He called me the next day. We have ended up being close friends to this day.

Be willing to say hello to someone new. My brother and his wife met at a concert. The important thing is to make the move on someone you are interested in, if they are not making a move on you. Be confident, the worst that could happen would be having to talk to a bore for a while.

Now that you've met this prospective candidate, get to know him or her, ask the questions that will reveal whether he or she possesses the qualities you prioritized. I recommend a lighthearted approach, so that he or she doesn't feel they are under a microscope (even though they are).

A strange and wonderful thing occurs when you start dating appropriate people. When you get to know someone who has both of your best interests at heart, the kind of relationship you will have becomes clear early on. What I mean is this: If you start dating someone who is a kind human being, but doesn't quite make your top five attribute list, that person might still become a good friend. They already want for you what you want for yourself. This is because they also want the same thing for themself–a fully functioning, thoroughly happy, totally committed, fulfilling love and family life. They know that unrequited love does not create happy situations, and so do you. The two of you have matured to the point where you've realized that you don't deserve to live in pain anymore–so if the relationship doesn't work, it's okay–they just aren't the "right one", and neither are you. This kind of maturity makes the letting go process a lot easier.

No matter what, if the person you are seeing doesn't match up to your list, use the bus analogy. Get off the bus and look for the next one.

Do be sensible with this step. There are some very unstable people out there. Be careful. Don't give out your home address to a stranger. At least find out who their friends are, and where they work.

Another very important part of this step is to clean up any past baggage related to marriage.

When I took this step, I decided to clean up every

relationship I ever had with every man in my life, starting with my father.

This is an ongoing process. It is not easy. A hint—forgiveness is a wonderful tool. So is compassion. However, if you have found yourself in the presence of a tyrant in your life, sometimes the best situation is to simply detach yourself from them.

I used to have a terrible time with the concept of detachment, especially from people who did not have my best interests at heart. It was difficult for me to conceive of evil. I really believe that people deep down are created noble and if you dig deep enough that nobility will show itself. Then it occurred to me one day that every one has free will, and like it or not there are some people who choose, for whatever reason, to be cruel. They can't help themselves, it is the way they have become. Until the time comes when they start experiencing more pain from their behavior than pleasure...they won't change. I realized that no matter how much I wanted to experience peace, love, harmony and unity...if the other person wasn't interested, or worse, was interested only in my debasement as a human being...it wasn't going to happen, and what I needed to do was not allow that person's experience of the world affect my experience of the universe. Then I found this quote from 'Abdúl-Bahá, someone I greatly respect and hope to emulate. "...Kindness cannot be shown the tyrant, the deceiver, or the thief, because far from awakening them to the error of their ways, it maketh them to continue in their perversity as before. No matter how much kindliness ye may expend upon the liar, he will but lie the more, for he believeth you to be deceived, while ye understand him but too well, and only remain silent out of your extreme compassion."[1]

After looking at my lousy track record of relationships strewn before my eyes, I realized that I kept having the same relationship over and over again. New name, new body, same situation; I knew I needed to heal old wounds. I was not satisfied in creating the same thing again. A good definition of craziness is; doing the same thing over and over expecting different results. I knew that if I was to earn my marriage certificate, I would have to honestly look my past relationships in the eye, and deal with my behavior. Since all the guys were basically the same (except one case which I'll get into later), my behavior was the only constant at which I had to look. What I saw was not pretty. My dad died when I was ten, and I had a big abandonment issue. Every time a man was interested in me, I was sure he would soon leave me. I was also very insecure about who I was.

This was my pattern. I'd meet someone. We'd hit it off and start spending time together—lots of phone calls, lots of intimate talk. Around the sixth week, I'd start changing, thinking I wasn't good enough the way I was, and I'd attempt to become the woman I thought he wanted me to be. That's when things would start going downhill. I would cry, be loving, be a bitch, whine, get self-deprecating and manipulate every situation to make it look like I was the wronged one. At that point neither one of us knew whether we were coming or going. Finally he would leave me to take a breather, and then just stay gone. And who could blame him, I was acting like an out of control, crazy woman!

Finding this out about myself was very helpful. I vowed not to repeat that behavior pattern. This time I would be myself and if he didn't like it, tough. In a nutshell, I wanted someone who would help foster my "good" qualities, and who would live with my "bad" habits and vice versa.

Now on to that exception I mentioned. A guy (who I will call Tom) who swept me off my feet, then dropped me big time from atop the "Empire State Building" (figuratively speaking). To put it plainly, I thought we were in love. I got pregnant. We talked about marriage and I was happier than I had ever been. Then one day he told me he couldn't be a father to anyone, and I had to get an abortion. He assured me that if I didn't I would end up on welfare. He said that all women were stupid to have children in the first place, especially his mother, and on and on. I was devastated. After considering my situation for a few weeks, I had the abortion. Within six weeks he married someone else. They divorced within the year.

This was my worst experience with a man.

During the process of clean-up I was able to effectively complete all my past relationships (without the luxury of having the man present) except the one with Tom. I felt it was imperative to deal with him one on one. I had moved away from California one year after we had broken up, and I had no idea how to get in contact with him. Years ago I heard that it only takes three contacts, be they letter, fax, or phone to contact any person no matter how obscure or famous so—I called an old friend of his whom I hadn't seen or heard from in three years. I asked him if he had heard from Tom and his friend told me he hadn't heard from him in over two years. I said if he happened to run into Tom, to please give him my phone number, and ask him to call me. This was on Thursday, May 25, 1989, the Thursday before Memorial Day Weekend. On Tuesday, May 30, I got a phone call from Tom at 8:00am. He and our mutual friend had run into each other on the street while vacationing in a small town during the long weekend. The possibility of running into someone you know, but haven't seen in years is always nice but this chance meeting seemed to me extremely improbable. I'm telling you, the power of your word is the most powerful force you have. To make a long story shorter, we absolutely completed our relationship, in that telephone call. I told him what I had come to believe, that if I never married and never had a child, I was warmed by the fact that somewhere in the universe there was a child that came through me and that child wouldn't be in God's world if it wasn't for us. Then I waited for his reply. He didn't even remember that I had been pregnant let alone had an abortion that he paid for! At that moment I knew without any reservation that I had done the right thing by having the abortion. I also saw that if Tom and I chose to continue a relationship with each other, it would be a new one. I was going to be in California later that summer and I made a date to see him in order to give him a book. More on that later. After the phone call with Tom I felt cleaner than I had been in my whole life. I felt that now nothing could stop me.

You are changing. You may find that people and things may be holding you back. Let them go. You may want to have a garage sale, give an old reminder away, or throw it out. Get rid of some of the photos in your photograph album of people who no longer belong there.

This process of taking responsibility for your future and letting go of your past will allow you to alter your personal history, thus truly preparing yourself for marriage.

CHAPTER EIGHT

A CONDOM IS NOT A PLACE WHERE YOU LIVE.

At this point I'd like to interject my thoughts about sex. Sex is wonderful however, it can also be a deterrent in finding out about a person's character. Let's face it, if the sex is good enough we will overlook just about any character flaw.

Doug and I waited until after we had set a wedding date to have sex. I was later told by a good friend of his that even though the lack of sexual relations frustrated him, that he understood, respected and loved me for it. I'll be honest—it frustrated me too. I had been consciously celibate for 5 1/2 years before I met Doug. When he hugged me, every nerve in my body went off. I felt like popcorn, popping! I wanted him. What is more important though, I wanted a healthy relationship, so we waited.

Total sexual intimacy requires commitment, trust and vulnerability. Trust takes time. After a couple marries, they continually grow together and this motivates them to find ways to satisfy each other sexually. If you attempt to share a sexual union with more than one person at a time, I believe you are cheating yourself of this intimacy. If you are not sure that the person sitting across the table from you is "the one" there are other, very creative ways to show affection without involving sex. You can speak to your beloved with kindness, compassion and affection. You can swim, write, watch a sunset together, or go house hunting. There are many ways two people can show affection without sexual contact. Show some imagination and I'm sure you will find some ways of your own. There are other reasons to wait for sex as well. For example, if you don't have memories of sex you don't have to get over them.

I had one relationship during my period of celibacy when I was engaged to someone other than Doug. Two weeks before the wedding was to take place he informed me that he couldn't marry me because he was untrustworthy. He told me that he had a male lover and had been with many men during our relationship. To put it mildly…I felt like the biggest fool under the sun.

As you can see celibacy protected me in more ways

than one. When we broke up, I was able to get over him quicker than relationships in which I had been physically intimate, because I didn't have the memories of physical intimacy to put behind me. I wasn't tormented by remembering the great sex, because there wasn't any. Also, three years after we broke up, he passed away from Valley Fever, complicated by AIDS.

This leads me to my next point. If you haven't been tested for AIDS, get tested. Do not have intimate relations with anyone without protection, and know the results of your potential partners' test. If you haven't been tested, suggest that the two of you get tested together before things go too far in your relationship. This is an issue of life and death, and must be addressed. If your potential partner is not willing to get tested, they are showing no consideration for your well being, or theirs, so STOP SEEING THEM. If one or both of you test positive, you have some serious decisions to make.

CHAPTER NINE

HOW TO MAKE YOUR MARRIAGE LAST FOREVER

16

C hoose healthy role models to follow if you want your marriage to last. If you are look-ing for a happy marriage look for couples who are happily married–a relationship you respect. Spend time with them. Ask them questions. Observe them. Find the qualities you appreciate in them and make them your own.

I chose a number of role models from friends of mine. I will call the three couples Couple A, Couple B and Couple C.

When I knew Couple A they had been married for 50 years. They had lived all over the world from Utah to Swaziland, to Haifa. Whenever Mr. A would tell a joke, Mrs. A would laugh the loudest. It didn't matter that she had heard the joke 100 times before. She loved, and respected her husband, they lived their lives like every day was new, so when she heard that joke, it was as if she had heard it for the first time. Mr. A was a prominent figure in their community and whenever he spoke publicly he always acknowledged Mrs. A as his strength. I remember asking her about their marriage. She told me it was very hard work to maintain a marriage, but definitely worth the adventure and spiritual growth it takes.

Couple B is perhaps the closest married couple to me. Mr. B is an engineer and Mrs. B is an author, business consultant and entrepreneur. Almost every Sunday for four years I would go to their home for dinner and a movie. They are perhaps the most generous couple I've ever met. They always hosted holiday parties for both their single and married friends. They were always there for me in an emergency (once I hurt my back, and they took me to the chiropractor in the middle of the night!). Through all their generosity and fun the one thing that became obvious to me after knowing them for a while is how much they truly love each other. They have been married since 1981 and they believe that the secret to a happy marriage is basic compatibility, a healthy dose of humor, and a good therapist. Mrs. B also believes that it is very important to be selfish and committed to your own personal growth as well as your partners.

Couple C is a wild couple. When I knew them he was 70 years old and she was in her early 40's. They believe in complete honesty. In fact they believe and live the idea that unless you can be completely honest, you probably don't feel loved. This concept changed my life. If you don't feel like you can tell your loved ones everything because you are afraid they won't love you if they know the real you, then you don't really feel loved by them. Withholding the truth or a feeling you have from your lover can be relationship suicide. On some level they know you aren't telling them something, and they most likely will think the worst, when it was really something as benign as "Gee, honey I hate it when you fold my socks that way." Couple C taught me a lot about being loved, and trusting the process of life. They taught me about compassion from a personal point of view. Because of meeting them I am a softer, kinder person.

On the other hand, you do not want to choose as role models couples that belittle each other, show no respect for one another, and generally dislike each other. This may seem obvious but I can tell you there are a lot more couples out there who you might think at first glance are having a great marriage because they don't argue and fight. These marriages could actually be falling apart simply because they don't communicate.

I lived with what I thought was the perfect couple for six weeks. Their children are precious, and the couple rarely fought. They seemed to communicate well. He was always saying that she was his best friend. Well, a few months after I got married, they separated. I couldn't believe it. He said he wasn't in love with her anymore. She didn't see it coming. It destroyed her life and her trust for a long time. A year later he married someone else.

Just because a couple doesn't argue and fight doesn't mean they have a stable relationship. In fact, sometimes just the opposite. Now I'm not talking knock-down drag-out fights where people get injured I'm talking about the clash of differing opinions. I believe it is a healthy thing when spouses have their own opinions and aren't afraid to voice them to each other. It makes for interesting conversation and dynamic personal growth.

CHAPTER TEN

THE LAW OF ATTRACTION

Congratulations!!! You are something special. Treat yourself to the pleasure of your choice. You have accomplished what most people only dream. You are a person who keeps commitments. You are trustworthy and dedicated. This is the point in the process where the steps reach a transition.

Let's go over what you've accomplished so far. You've asked yourself why you want to get married–a question few people ever ask. You've declared what you want and by what date you will have it. You have even gone so far as to write it down on paper. By doing this you have taken complete responsibility for your future. You have written down all the attributes you want your mate to possess. You've read your list nine times consecutively over a three day period and burned it to let it go. You are telling as many people as you can that you will be married and by what date. You are establishing credibility for yourself by keeping the commitments you make. You are willing to take whatever steps are necessary to get married. You are putting yourself out in the marketplace. You are taking responsibility for your past relationships (which is something that even fewer people ever do).

Up to this point you have laid a foundation, now it's time to build the house. What I mean by this is–a big chunk of the work has been done–you can only continue this process of goal setting and effective action and have faith; faith in yourself to accomplish your goal; faith in the Universe to supply the means by which to achieve it; and faith in your partner to show up within the designated time. This does not mean that now you get to sit back, watch TV and wait for some stranger to knock on your door to marry you. You must continue to make yourself available.

I actually chose to have a "relationship coach". I chose someone who I thought despite all odds met and married a wonderful man. I chose her because she represented to me a person who was successful in the area of personal relationships and she was someone who believed in me. When she accepted the position, I thought she would have lots of good advice and words of wisdom. She ended up telling me only one thing. She said, "Be attractive". This stupefied me. Be attractive? What did that mean? She was a hair dresser who always had her hair coifed and her make-up perfectly applied. That is not my style. Surely she couldn't mean that I needed a make-over. "What is she talking about?", I thought. It wasn't as though I was completely unattractive. I knew my looks would be desirable to at least a select few.

I searched my heart for the meaning of "being attractive." I was the one being shallow. Her statement was actually very profound. I started seeing myself as a magnet for my mate, not only physically but mentally, emotionally, and spiritually. I started visualizing myself as attracting within my field the one who would be my partner. This gave me a sense of great relief. If I were a magnet for "husband" that meant I would repel "non husband". Well, it worked for me.

Find yourself a relationship coach. Someone **you trust.** Someone who sees you honestly and will tell you the truth in a way you can hear. Now is the time to act with tireless, ceaseless energy. Act as if the goal has already been accomplished.

CHAPTER ELEVEN

WHAT HAPPENS IF EVERYTHING I'VE DONE SO FAR DOESN'T WORK?

Okay, so you've done everything I've prescribed so far in this book and not only are you not married yet, you still haven't met anyone remotely qualified for the position. Even though your goal date has not arrived, if you are feeling frustrated and your thinking is going along the lines of... "This is ridiculous, this plan isn't working, whatever made me think that I could attract a mate, this book is stupid..." It is a good time to ask yourself the question: "What if I don't get married?"

It is very important to explore this as a real possibility. By this exploration you will learn how attached you are to the idea of getting married. That very attachment may be what is getting in your way. Herein lies the catch. In order for this step to be successful you must approach it openly, directly and sincerely, for its own sake. If you approach the question with the idea of getting it over with so you can get married, it won't work.

*When I asked myself this question it was July 1989. I was floating by myself, in the ocean, and the thought hit me, "What if I **don't** get married?" My mind went blank. It was as if I blacked out for a moment. Then, I started to weep. Not only did I not know the answer to the question… I couldn't even "be" with the question! So I asked again—same reaction. I asked once more, and more tears came. "This is ridiculous.", I thought. Then something came over me. I realized that I was so attached, so invested in getting my goal I couldn't allow for any other possibility. I felt this wasn't healthy. I truly believe that until you can detach yourself from your goal, you will not achieve it in happiness.*

I decided to make a sub-goal. My new sub-goal was to be able to ask myself the question, "What if I don't get married," and be conscious enough to "be" with the question for a few minutes.

Please read the question accurately. This question is not "What if I don't get married by my goal date" it is "What if I don't get married?" period, end of chapter.

I asked myself this question a lot over the next several weeks. I gave myself permission to feel whatever would come up. I talked to people about it. Now when you talk to people, be picky. Choose people who will empower you in your life. If you don't have anyone like that...hire someone. Sometimes you just need someone to listen. Ultimately you will come to the answer on your own. This process of asking myself "The Question" took one month almost to the day. Then things really started moving.

When you can face this question, a transformation occurs. Dealing with a worst case scenario (and, for some, not getting married can seem like just that) can give you an incredible amount of freedom. This freedom allows you to see options and know that there are choices.

By facing this possibility, you have completed another part of the guide. It is time to trust and move forward. When there are more options, movement becomes more graceful. Deep inside you know that if you don't get married your life isn't over. It may not be what you had expected...but then again, it may lead to even more wonderful possibilities.

CHAPTER TWELVE

A POSSIBLE SOLUTION TO:
"WHAT HAPPENS IF EVERYTHING I'VE DONE
SO FAR DOESN'T WORK"

Now is a good time to create an alternate plan. One that is satisfying, not a booby prize. Remember, there are many possibilities to fulfill yourself as a person. The truth is—you do not need to marry in order to be whole. We've just been conditioned to feel that way. Create for yourself a life that is free from the complication of marriage. I have an acquaintance who decided to put her nursing skills to work in the Cayman Islands. Years later, she told me that her life changed the day she finally gave up on marriage. She said her friendships with men became deeper and more intimate once she stopped looking at them as "prospects" and started looking at them as people. When she turned forty, she decided to adopt the child of an Island friend. Apparently, in that culture if a family feels they have enough children, it is considered a great blessing to give the next one to a childless friend. Since this Island woman and her husband already had eight children they contracted to give the newborn to my friend. Tragically, the mother died from a complication in childbirth. The baby survived however, and one year later my friend married the baby's father. At forty-two, she became a wife, and mother of nine!

This woman's life is a perfect example of that irritating cliché people have been telling you your whole life. You know, the one that goes, "You'll find it when you aren't looking..." How do you not look for your heart's desire? You can't. You always look for your heart's desire, you just must stop limiting yourself to it.

Whatever it is that you choose for your alternate plan, make sure you are not compromising on your desire to make your life work. By creating an alternate plan to marriage you are giving your goal (of marriage) the freedom to be accomplished.

Now after all that you have just read, I want you to remember your declaration—the one you wrote down in this book on page 35... It reads, I (your name) will be married by (your date). I mean, you still want to get married, don't you? There is a possibility that you don't, but if you do still want to marry, read on to learn my alternate plan.

My alternate plan was to apply for a position at the International Headquarters of my faith in Israel. Once I created this alternative for my life (which was sometime in the middle of August 1989), I felt renewed. After all, I only had four and a half more months until my goal date. I knew I would either be married, starting a new life with my husband, or (if they offered me a position) making plans to go to Haifa, starting a new life in Israel, or maybe something even better that I didn't know about yet. Whatever would happen, I knew change was coming, and I was excited!

CHAPTER THIRTEEN

THESE TWO IMPORTANT INGREDIENTS WILL GUARANTEE SUCCESS

The two ingredients are faith and trust. A very wise man once said, "Have faith and confidence that the power will flow through you, the right way will appear, the door will open, the right thought, the right message [the right person], the right principal, or the right book will be given to you. Have confidence and the right thing will come to your need".[2] In other words, act as if your goal has already been accomplished. Trust that it has.

Trust is an important issue. This is the point where faith in the Universe and yourself comes into play. Your foundation is strong. Believe that the cosmos will supply you with the proper tool (mate) to build your house (marriage). A marriage is built on trust. By having faith in yourself, trusting another (your partner) will be easier. For if you don't trust yourself, can you really have faith in anyone else?

My faith came in a wonderful way. The second week of August 1989 I went on a retreat. I drove from Tucson, Arizona to Santa Cruz, California. I stopped the first night in Los Angeles to visit my mother. The next morning I was off to rendezvous with Tom the man from my past. You remember, the one who couldn't be a father? We were supposed to meet at a restaurant in Santa Barbara a town about 100 miles north of Los Angeles. He stood me up. Actually, I spied him from the parking lot. He was in a liquor store across the street from the restaurant in which we were to meet. I was early, and admittedly a bit nervous about seeing him again so I waited for him in the lobby of the restaurant and read while I waited for him. After twenty minutes I realized he was a no show, so I left. Then an interesting thing happened. I realized that in the past, I would have taken his action very personally. That day however, my thoughts ran towards pity for him. He had been offered a wonderful opportunity to fully complete our relationship for himself. He instead chose to have another in-complete scenario in his life. My next thought was that I was being protected from this unhealthy man.

Driving to the location of my retreat, I felt an energy

of impending fulfillment. I spent my 33rd birthday at the retreat and some of my fellow retreaters gave me a beautiful signed copy of "The Peace Bible." I felt loved and accepted.

This experience was in sharp contrast to my past. My first group experience in a camp-like setting was at summer camp at age ten. I always felt like the outcast. I was not popular. I was always the last one picked on any sports team and I was rarely asked to dance at the camp socials. One year my cabin voted to have me moved to another cabin. I came back from the swimming pool to find my bags packed and a note stating that they hoped I could find another empty bed for the remaining ten days of camp (I did find another empty bed in a cabin of other social rejects and started to have a pretty good time). As you can see, I was not always a happy, self-assured person. Because of this past experience the retreat was even more special.

A few days after my birthday, I decided to conduct my reading, meditation and prayer in the woods. It was there that it struck me...I was already married! The goal had been accomplished. I just hadn't caught up to it yet. Now, this was a radical thought, even for me. But as sure as I knew my name, I knew this was true. A new feeling of joy and confidence came over me. I left Santa Cruz two days later to go home to Tucson.

The first Saturday of every month, Tucson has a party. The city closes off several streets in the downtown arts district. All the galleries are open, there is street entertainment, and lots of people. *The Saturday Night of Labor Day Weekend (exactly one year from the date of my original declaration to marry), I went downtown to the party with a couple of friends and had a great time. There was a group of African dancers dancing in the streets. One of the dancers was on stilts. I was feeling very festive and found myself dancing with him. I passed under his legs and really abandoned myself to the dance. At one point, he looked me in the eye through his mask and said, "Soon you will marry." He didn't know me from Eve and he certainly didn't know whether or not I was married, but still he felt compelled to tell me this information. All I could reply was "I know," then I left him and joined my friends. The next day Doug called.*

CHAPTER FOURTEEN

Your Ideal Mate Already Knows
This About You.

By the time Doug called I was so detached about this marriage thing that I almost let him slip by. He phoned me on Sunday and asked if he could come over to use a piece of equipment I had from the flotation tank center. I told him I had sold the business and gave him the new owner's phone number. Then he said, "You mean you don't have the machine anymore?" I told him that I did, but for personal use only. He persisted, "Can't I come over tomorrow and use it with you there?" Well, the next day was Labor Day and I was going to a party. I said, "Give me a break! It's Labor Day and I'm taking the day off." I ended up begrudgingly giving him an appointment for the following Wednesday night.

The man who bought my business called Tuesday and told me Doug had come to a session, and that he talked about how much he was looking forward to seeing me. After Doug was described to me I remembered who he was, and got a little excited myself.

Doug came over Wednesday night at 10:00pm and we talked until 1:00am. Friday night we went out for a movie and dinner, went back to his apartment and talked until 2:00am. Sunday we got together around 5:00pm and talked until 3:00am. On Tuesday I went away for 10 days to a conference and my sister's wedding. I called Doug once from the conference and we talked for about half an hour. I felt the 10 day separation was good for us. It gave me some breathing space—but I must admit Doug was on my mind and in my heart. When I came home from my sister's wedding I went directly to Doug's apartment. We went out for dinner and he told me that while I was gone, a woman he used to know wanted to have sex with him. He told me that while he was tempted—he knew intuitively that if he did go out with her that would be the end of our relationship. He told me what he wanted was to be in a committed relationship with me.

My point is, if it wasn't for Doug's persistence I might have overlooked him. DON'T DO THAT!!! If you think you might, add tenacity to the list of attributes for your mate.

Occasionally you need to step back and look objectively at the place you are in your life. Have you been spending a lot of time with just one person? Are you investigating their character? Does this person have the top five qualities on your list? If so, how many other qualities do they have? What qualities don't they possess? Of those qualities, are they truly and objectively important, or could they be blocks holding you back? If this person has the important qualities, and assuming they feel the same about you, CONGRATULATIONS! You may have found your mate.

CHAPTER FIFTEEN

The Beginning At Last

Once you've found your mate you have a lot to celebrate—but you may not realize it right away. Sure you've accomplished your goal, but you've accomplished a lot more than that too. You've grown in a direction of your choosing. You have opened up to new possibilities and let go of old limitations from your past that previously held you back. Don't be surprised if it takes a while for that to sink in.

The day after Doug and I decided to marry I was talking with a girlfriend, and when I told her we were engaged, she shrieked with happiness. My reaction was a bit more subdued. I actually felt incredibly sober. I always thought that when that moment occurred I would be on top of the world, yelling from the roof-

tops. You know, like in the movies. The reality, for me, was different. Not only was I engaged to be married but I had reached what most people considered for me, an unattainable goal. After all I was over 30, college educated, independent, a small business owner, and fat. Even my mother had lost faith in the idea of marriage for me. It wasn't until I let the idea sink in a bit that I started getting excited. It took me four days to gather enthusiasm over the idea of getting married.

Now you have found your heart's desire, the person to share your life with. If you decide to marry, set the date (please not too far in the future), discuss your future plans, and celebrate your miracle.

CHAPTER SIXTEEN

A FINAL NOTE

A very wise woman told me, "Kalyn, when you choose the man you want to marry, spend a week with his family. Beyond all other things notice how your intended treats his mother, because one day, that is how he will treat you." The mother-son, father-daughter relationship is a precious one. Whether one's parents treated them with respect and honesty or disrespect and cruelty, that primary relationship shapes one's life in a very profound way. A son finds his success method for dealing with the opposite sex from his mother and a daughter from her father. When a little girl flirts with her father she gets messages of approval or disapproval from her daddy. Later on when it comes time to flirt with boys, she relies on the response she received from her father to show her the way.

When I was a little girl I flirted outrageously with my dad. I still flirt today, it's fun. I also see in my own life how my father's death still affects me in how I deal with my husband. In times of stress I revert to being a little girl. I throw temper tantrums and sometimes, throw objects (nothing big and never at anyone). I think because I was left with no father or father figure at a young age I never had the benefit of learning how to deal with conflict and stress in my intimate relationships with men as an adult. I noticed at the beginning of my marriage with Doug that in times of stress, he treated me with indifference. Well, guess what—that's how he treated his mother. A male relative of mine treats his mother with complete disrespect and dishonor. When he married his wife he treated her like a queen, but after several years of marriage and lots of stress we all noticed that he treats her just like he treats his mother. On the other hand, a male friend of mine (after lots of family therapy) has had a pretty healthy relationship with his mother for years, and after several years of marriage he still treats her with respect and devotion.

The reason I am putting this chapter in the book is that I know you don't just want to get married, but that you want the best relationship you can have. I want you to gather as many tools as you can to build a strong and loving home with your spouse, in order to build a strong, loving, and devoted family. Remember at the beginning of the book when I told you I am committed to seeing divorce decline in the United States, in new marriages, by 35% by the year 2000? Well one of the ways I see that happening is through education. When we start marrying not only for love, and passion but because we find our best friend sitting across the table from us we may accomplish the task of healthy relationships. When we **choose** to spend the rest of our life growing with that person no matter what—then we will start to experience true equality, liberty and lots of fun in our home life. I once saw a needlepoint picture at a friend's home—it said "Choose thy love...and love thy choice" I have included a rendering of it at the end of this book for you to copy or color or whatever.

We are the first generation ever that has the tools to create powerful relationships beyond our wildest dreams. I also feel however, that as a generation we got the short end of the stick. We are the first generation not to do as well materially as our parents. Environmentally we are choking from the chemicals in our air, food, and water. The legacy that has been left to us as far as relationships is also pretty dismal. Dysfunction is the norm. That doesn't mean, however, that we have to remain victims of our forefathers' carelessness. It means that we can have the bounty of being responsible for a whole new world order. We have an opportunity to make things any way we choose. We can choose health or let dysfunction continue into the next generation. Let's do the next generation a favor and give them a gift at the same time. Let's give them wonderful role models to follow and parental relationships they want to emulate. Let's not just do it for ourselves...let's do it for our children.

AFTERWORD

I know that my story contains good timing and what appears to be magic but, isn't that what life's miracles are all about? Once you have mastered the declaration/goal process you will find it works in all areas of your life. For example: When I got out of college, and moved back to Los Angeles in 1977 I told everyone that I would find a one bedroom courtyard apartment for no more that $150.00 a month by my birthday. Everyone thought I was crazy. At that time you couldn't find an apartment in a decent neighborhood for under $200.00 a month—but I did it. I repeated the exercise in 1981 for an apartment in one of the canyons of Los Angeles for $200.00 a month. Everyone else was paying at least

$350.00. Shortly after our wedding (about an hour to be precise), friends started asking us when we would start our family. I said I wanted to be pregnant before I was 35 between May and August 1991. Then on our wedding night Doug said, "Wouldn't it be great if we had twins and got the whole thing over with in one fell swoop?". Well, there are no twins on either side of our families but, it was my wedding night and I was feeling pretty festive so I said, "Sure honey, that would be great!" Our twins were born April, 29, 1992. I conceived a few days before my 35th birthday in August 1991. I'm telling you, this stuff really works!

One more thing before I go...now that you've read this guide, please let me know how it affects you. You can contact me at:

Just Your Type
Publishing & Marketing
P.O. Box 5931
Eugene, OR 97405
(503) 683-4149
(503) 484-2663 fax

I'm truly interested...may you always walk in Peace and Unity.

Kalyn Wolf Gibbens

ENDNOTES

1. Pages 66-67, 'Abdú'l-Bahá: The Divine Art of Living, Selections from the Writings of Bahá'u'lláh and 'Abdú'l-Bahá, 1986, Bahá'í Publishing Trust Wilmette, Illinois.

2. Page 91, Shoghi Effendi: Dynamics of Prayer for Solving Problems, Bahá'í Prayer Book, Revised Edition 1985, Bahá'í Publishing Trust Committee, Bahá'ís of Malaysia.

SUGGESTED READING

"A Fortress for Well-Being", 1973 National Spiritual
Assembly of the Bahá'ís of the United States.
*A wonderful book on marriage. When Doug asked me what I
was looking for in a marriage, I handed him this book and said,
"This about covers it."*

"How to be a Couple and Still be Free", Tina Tessina and
Riley Smith, 1980, Newcastle Publishing Co., Inc.
*This book showed me that marriage does not have to mean "ball
and chain".*

"Women Who Love Too Much", Robin Norwood, 1985,
Jeremy Tarcher, Inc.
*If you think you might be co-dependent read this book. If you
don't think you are, read this book anyway it couldn't hurt.*

"The Kin of Ata Are Waiting for You", Dorothy Bryant,
1971, Random House
I love this book. It will enlighten and delight you.

"If I'm So Wonderful, Why Am I Still Single", Susan Page,
1988, Viking
*Doug recommends this book. It gave him a no nonsense,
straightforward approach to placing himself in situations where
he'd be more likely to find his mate (me).*

"How to Get the Love You Want", Harville Hendrix, 1988,
Harper & Row
*As far as I'm concerned this is **the** book to read in regards to
understanding and implementing the healing of childhood wounds
for having a conscious marriage. READ THIS BOOK!*

INDEX

113

FORMS
(FOR A FRIEND)

PLEASE SEND

MARRYING SMART
A PRACTICAL GUIDE FOR ATTRACTING YOUR MATE

TO MY FRIEND
TO ORDER CALL (503) 683-4149

☐ Please send this gift anonymously

☐ Please put this note with the gift:

_____

_____

_____

Friend's Name _____

Address _____

City _____

State _____ Zip _____

Phone ( ) _____

My Name _____

Credit Card # _____

Expiration date _____

Name on card _____

Signature _____

Phone ( ) _____

Please send a check or money order for $10.95 + $3.50 shipping and handling to:

Just Your Type Publishing & Marketing
PO Box 5931
Eugene, OR 97405

VISA°

MasterCard

You may copy this form for additional orders.

FORMS
(ADDITIONAL COPIES)

PLEASE SEND ME
ADDITIONAL COPIES OF

MARRYING SMART
A PRACTICAL GUIDE FOR ATTRACTING YOUR MATE

TO ORDER CALL (503) 683-4149

☐ Please send me _____ additional copies of Marrying Smart

Name _____

Address _____

City _____

State _____ Zip _____

Phone ( ) _____

My Name _____

Please send a check or money order for $10.95 for each book. Shipping and Handling is $3.50 for the first book and $1.00 for each additional book.

Mail to:
Just Your Type Publishing & Marketing
PO Box 5931
Eugene, OR 97405

VISA·

MasterCard

Credit Card # _____

Expiration date _____

Name on card _____

Signature _____

You may copy this form for additional orders.

FORMS
(COMMENTS AND EXPERIENCES)

PLEASE SEND
YOUR COMMENTS AND EXPERIENCES
FROM
MARRYING SMART
A PRACTICAL GUIDE FOR ATTRACTING YOUR MATE
DIRECTLY TO KALYN*

*ALL COMMENTS BECOME THE PROPERTY OF JUST YOUR TYPE PUBLISHING & MARKETING

Dear Kalyn:

_____

_____

_____

_____

_____

_____

_____

_____

_____

_____

_____

My Name _____

City _____

State _____

Telephone(   ) _____

You can fax this form to: (503) 484-2663 or you can mail it to:

Kalyn Wolf Gibbens
PO Box 5931
Eugene, OR 97405

FORMS
(EXTENDED INTEREST)

I'm Ready To Marry Smart!

Kalyn, will you be my relationships coach?

I am available to take on a limited amount of people who are sincere about wanting to get married the SMART way. If you are interested in working with me check one or all of the following boxes and I'll get back with you soon:

☐ Yes! I want to work with you on a one-on-one basis.

☐ Yes! I'd be interested in conference call coaching sessions along with other SMART people like me.

☐ I'd be interested in planning a Marrying Smart seminar or workshop in my area.

Name _____

Address _____

City _____

State _____ Zip _____

Phone ( ) _____

You can fax this form to: (503) 484-2663 or you can mail this form to:

Kalyn Wolf Gibbens
PO Box 5931
Eugene, OR 97405

You may copy this form for additional orders.

NOTES

NOTES